With a Friend

by Your Side

Barbara Kerley

NATIONAL
GEOGRAPHIC

WASHINGTON, D.C.

There, in the crowd, is **someone**—

who **likes** the things you like

who **thinks** the way you do

who finds the same **jokes** funny

who wants to **meet you**, too.

So, **step** right up. Don't be shy.

Imagine what can happen with a **friend** by your side.

Friends are great for

getting **goofy**

being **brave**

sharing **secrets**

sharing **snacks**.

They're just who you want

when you need a **quick hug**

at the end of a not-so-great day.

They give you a **boost**

and save you a **seat**.

They **carry** the other end.

They **clap** the hardest
and **cheer** the loudest.

They like having you for a **friend**.

With a friend by your side you can go a little **farther**

reach a little **higher**

dig in your heels and try a little **harder**.

You can step up and

stand tall **together**.

All you need is a **friend** by your side.

Friends Around the World

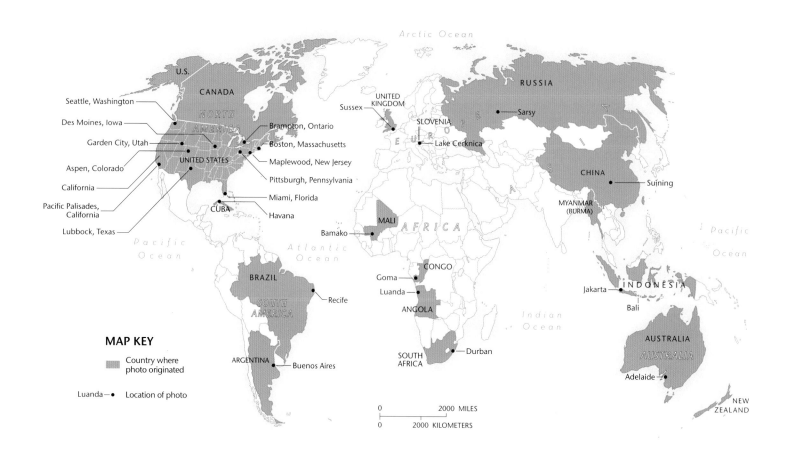

Arctic Ocean

U.S.

CANADA

NORTH AMERICA

Seattle, Washington

Des Moines, Iowa

Garden City, Utah

Aspen, Colorado

California

Pacific Palisades, California

Lubbock, Texas

UNITED STATES

Brampton, Ontario

Boston, Massachusetts

Maplewood, New Jersey

Pittsburgh, Pennsylvania

Miami, Florida

CUBA

Havana

Pacific Ocean

Atlantic Ocean

BRAZIL

SOUTH AMERICA

Recife

ARGENTINA

Buenos Aires

UNITED KINGDOM

Sussex

SLOVENIA

Lake Cerknica

EUROPE

AFRICA

MALI

Bamako

CONGO

Goma

Luanda

ANGOLA

SOUTH AFRICA

Durban

RUSSIA

Sarsy

ASIA

CHINA

Suining

MYANMAR (BURMA)

Indian Ocean

INDONESIA

Jakarta

Bali

Pacific Ocean

AUSTRALIA

Adelaide

NEW ZEALAND

MAP KEY

Country where photo originated

Luanda — ● Location of photo

0   2000 MILES

0   2000 KILOMETERS

Taking a leap in
Garden City, Utah, U.S.A.

Not feeling blue at all in
Buenos Aires, Argentina

Cooling off in
Suining, China

Hunting the next great wave
in **California, U.S.A.**

Sharing a treat in
Sussex, United Kingdom

Thinking inside the box in
New Zealand

Being zany in
Des Moines, Iowa, U.S.A.

Sharing a laugh in
Bali, Indonesia

Holding hands in
Lubbock, Texas, U.S.A.

A leafy peek in
Seattle, Washington, U.S.A.

Seeing eye to eye in
Aspen, Colorado, U.S.A.

Rinsing off in
Boston, Massachusetts, U.S.A.

Clowning around in
Bamako, Mali

Slip sliding down a muddy hill near
Jakarta, Indonesia

A meeting of the minds
in the **United Kingdom**

Time for snacks in
Brampton, Ontario, Canada

Propping each other up in
Goma, Congo

Being tall in
Adelaide, Australia

Loving the library
in the **United States**

Working as a team in
Miami, Florida, U.S.A.

Celebrating a win in
Durban, South Africa

Joining together in
Pittsburgh, Pennsylvania, U.S.A.

Playing cards in
Bamako, Mali

Being adventurous in
Maplewood, New Jersey, U.S.A.

Getting ready to fly in
Pacific Palisades, California, U.S.A.

Scoring a GOAAAAL in
Luanda, Angola

All lined up and ready
to go in **Myanmar**

About to get wet in
Lake Cerknica, Slovenia

Finding a friend in
Havana, Cuba

Cozying up to a good book in
Sarsy, Russia

Speaking the same language
in the **United States**

Leaning on each other
in **Canada**

Dancing on the beach in
Recife, Brazil

Friends come in all shapes, sizes, ages, and colors.

Think about the things you like about yourself. Are you:

sweet **funny** smart
athletic kind **calm**
curious strong
serious outgoing happy
inventive **loud**
fun **helpful** silly
creative active quiet ?

What other words describe you? These are some of the qualities that make you who you are.

You can find great qualities in all sorts of other people who may look very different—on the outside—than you do. Your pets have great qualities, too! When you meet someone, it's good to keep an open mind about who they are inside. You might be surprised to see what qualities they have and who ends up being a friend.

And remember: You may not become close friends with everyone you meet, but you can treat everyone with kindness and respect—qualities that help make you a good friend!

—Barbara Kerley

"The only way to have a friend **is to be one.**"

—Ralph Waldo Emerson

. . . .

"**Friendship is born** at the **moment** when one man says to another, 'What! **You too?** I thought that no one but myself . . .'"

—C. S. Lewis

friend *(n):*
pal, buddy,
partner,
supporter,
colleague, ally,
companion, chum,
mate, well-wisher,
playmate, sidekick,
soul mate

For **parents** and **caregivers**

We all know the importance of making and retaining friendships. The best way to help our children be good friends is to set an example by showing kindness and respect toward others.

Don't be afraid to talk to your kids about bullying so they recognize and understand it and so that they know what to do when confronted with it. Keep communicating with your children and, of course, encourage them to do what they love.

For ideas on helping your kids make friends, see
- http://kids.nationalgeographic.com/friend
- www.pbs.org/parents/education/going-to-school/social/make-new-friends
- http://www.webmd.com/parenting/family-health-12/child-make-friends

For more resources on bullying, see
- http://education.nationalgeographic.com/education/news/teaching-tolerance/?ar_a=1
- www.stopbullying.gov
- http://www.nea.org/home/neabullyfree.html

"Friendship is a **sheltering** tree."
—Samuel Taylor Coleridge

For Karlyn

Staff for This Book
Erica Green, *Senior Editor*
Amanda Larsen, *Art Director and Designer*
Lori Epstein, *Senior Photo Editor*
Paige Towler, *Editorial Assistant*
Allie Allen and Sanjida Rashid, *Design Production Assistants*
Michael Cassady, *Photo Assistant*
Carl Mehler, *Director of Maps*
Grace Hill, *Associate Managing Editor*
Mike O'Connor, *Production Editor*
Lewis R. Bassford, *Production Manager*
Robert L. Barr, *Manager, Production Services*
Susan Borke, *Legal and Business Affairs*

Published by the National Geographic Society
Gary E. Knell, *President and CEO*
John M. Fahey, *Chairman of the Board*
Melina Gerosa Bellows, *Chief Education Officer*
Declan Moore, *Chief Media Officer*
Hector Sierra, *Senior Vice President and General Manager, Book Division*

Senior Management Team, Kids Publishing and Media
Nancy Laties Feresten, *Senior Vice President;* Jennifer Emmett, *Vice President, Editorial Director, Kids Books;* Julie Vosburgh Agnone, *Vice President, Editorial Operations;* Rachel Buchholz, *Editor and Vice President,* NG Kids *magazine;* Michelle Sullivan, *Vice President, Kids Digital;* Eva Absher-Schantz, *Design Director;* Jay Sumner, *Photo Director;* Hannah August, *Marketing Director;* R. Gary Colbert, *Production Director*

Digital
Anne McCormack, *Director;* Laura Goertzel, Sara Zeglin, *Producers;* Jed Winer, *Special Projects Assistant;* Emma Rigney, *Creative Producer;* Brian Ford, *Video Producer;* Bianca Bowman, *Assistant Producer;* Natalie Jones, *Senior Product Manager*

The National Geographic Society is one of the world's largest nonprofit scientific and educational organizations. Founded in 1888 to "increase and diffuse geographic knowledge," the Society's mission is to inspire people to care about the planet. It reaches more than 400 million people worldwide each month through its official journal, *National Geographic,* and other magazines; National Geographic Channel; television documentaries; music; radio; films; books; DVDs; maps; exhibitions; live events; school publishing programs; interactive media; and merchandise. National Geographic has funded more than 10,000 scientific research, conservation, and exploration projects and supports an education program promoting geographic literacy.

For more information, please visit nationalgeographic.com, call 1-800-NGS LINE (647-5463), or write to the following address:
National Geographic Society
1145 17th Street N.W.
Washington, D.C. 20036-4688 U.S.A.

Visit us online at nationalgeographic.com/books

For librarians and teachers: ngchildrensbooks.org

More for kids from National Geographic: kids.nationalgeographic.com

For information about special discounts for bulk purchases, please contact National Geographic Books Special Sales: ngspecsales@ngs.org

For rights or permissions inquiries, please contact National Geographic Books Subsidiary Rights: ngbookrights@ngs.org

Hardcover ISBN: 978-1-4263-1905-1
Reinforced library binding ISBN: 978-1-4263-1906-8

Printed in Hong Kong
14/THK/1